Saving the Night

HOW LIGHT POLLUTION IS HARMING LIFE ON EARTH

STEPHEN AITKEN

ORCA BOOK PUBLISHERS

Text copyright © Stephen Aitken 2023

Published in Canada and the United States in 2023
by Orca Book Publishers.
orcabook.com

Library and Archives Canada Cataloguing in Publication
Title: Saving the night : how light pollution is harming life on Earth /
Stephen Aitken.
Names: Aitken, Stephen, 1953- author.
Series: Orca footprints.
Description: Series statement: Orca footprints |
Includes bibliographical references and index.
Identifiers: Canadiana (print) 20220211183 |
Canadiana (ebook) 20220211191 | ISBN 9781459831070 (hardcover) |
ISBN 9781459831087 (PDF) | ISBN 9781459831094 (EPUB)
Subjects: LCSH: Light pollution—Juvenile literature.
Classification: LCC QB51.3.L53 A48 2023 | DDC j522—dc23

Library of Congress Control Number: 2022935255

Summary: This nonfiction book introduces middle-grade readers to the effects of light pollution. Illustrated with photos throughout, it discusses why darkness is important for plants, animals and people, and the practical things we can do to protect the night sky for all ecosystems on the planet.

Orca Book Publishers is committed to reducing the consumption of nonrenewable resources in the production of our books. We make every effort to use materials that support a sustainable future.

Orca Book Publishers gratefully acknowledges the support for its publishing programs provided by the following agencies: the Government of Canada, the Canada Council for the Arts and the Province of British Columbia through the BC Arts Council and the Book Publishing Tax Credit.

Front cover photos by Fabio Palmieri / EyeEm/Getty Images and Roman Becker / EyeEm/Getty Images.
Back cover photos by Kirill Ryzhov/Dreamstime.com, Johanna Turner and Pere Sanz/Dreamstime.com.
Design by Teresa Bubela
Layout by Jenn Playford
Edited by Kirstie Hudson

Printed and bound in South Korea.

26 25 24 23 • 1 2 3 4

The stars are huge celestial bodies, but they are light-years away from Earth, appearing as tiny sparkling dots in our night sky.
SARAYUT THANEERAT/GETTY IMAGES

To my parents, for the nights we lived on the land of Feadán

Contents

CHAPTER ONE
NIGHT AND DAY IN THE NATURAL WORLD

CHAPTER TWO
ARTIFICIAL LIGHTS ON LAND

CHAPTER THREE
LIGHTING THE OCEANS, LAKES AND RIVERS

CHAPTER FOUR
GUARDIANS OF THE NIGHT

Introduction

The air is different at night, cooler and laden with riches. Strange, unfamiliar sounds seem louder. Sweet, fragrant scents hang in the humid night air. As you walk into the darkness, your eyes slowly adjust to the dim light. You instinctively reach for a flashlight. But wait. Avoid that reflex. The outline of the nearby trees slowly starts to appear. Stars sparkle above in the deep, dark sky.

Imagine you're standing in the middle of the Milky Way. You look off to the outer arms of the galaxy and a pale blue dot appears out of the darkness. It's our planet Earth, a mere speck of dust spinning in a sunbeam. Now zoom in, all the way in. Life on Earth has evolved in both daylight and darkness over billions of years, in dense jungles, on rolling desert sands, in deep ocean waters and in shallow coral reefs. Monkeys, owls, fungi, rodents, frogs, salamanders and bats have adapted to life in the darkness. They mate, forage for food, build shelters and, most important, avoid the hungry jaws of their predators.

This view of Earth from space captures the sunrise over North America. Clusters of lights are seen illuminating cities all night long.
RANGIZZZ/DREAMSTIME.COM

Amphibians like this tree frog have adapted to nights that range from complete darkness to full moonlight. Scientists speculate that artificial lights, shown to disrupt amphibian life cycles, may lead to population declines. MOMO5287/SHUTTERSTOCK.COM

I was afraid of the dark until I was seven years old. The basement in our new house terrified me. But slowly the night sky outside promised more riches than fright. I grew to love the night—the thrill of standing alone in a field of chirping crickets, the haunting hoots of owls resonating through the trees of the forests nearby.

But the dark night I knew is rapidly changing. In only seven or eight human generations since the invention of the light bulb, the world at night has become flooded with light. One by one the celestial bodies are disappearing as the night sky is bleached by the glow of city lights. Light spills into *ecosystems* that harbor animals, insects and plants long adapted to dark nights. Artificial lights have become another form of pollution imposed on our living planet, which is already teetering from the activity of close to eight billion people. This book explores some of the most serious effects of light pollution and the determined conservationists who are working to save the night.

It is in our hands to decide how we use lights at night. Only we can minimize the impact of lighting on people as well as on nocturnal animals and insects.
ATIT SIRIPRAROB/SHUTTERSTOCK.COM

CHAPTER ONE

Night and Day in the Natural World

NIGHT ON EARTH

Colorful waves of northern lights dance over this Icelandic scene. High-energy particles from the sun strike the earth's magnetic field and are redirected to the poles, causing the beautiful aurora borealis.
SIMON'S PASSION 4 TRAVEL/SHUTTERSTOCK.COM

Our star, the sun, started shining over four and a half billion years ago. It burns nonstop, 24 hours a day, giving energy to our entire solar system. But what about the night? You may have heard that our planet orbits the sun while spinning around at a thousand miles per hour. At any point in time, half of the earth is illuminated by the sun while the other half lies in darkness. Well, not exactly *complete* darkness. The earth has a natural satellite—the moon. The moon is like a gift from the sun to the night, its rough, rocky surface reflecting about 8 percent of the sunlight reaching it. Starlight, *zodiacal light* and *airglow* cut back the darkness even further. This gentle glow of the night sky has long inspired poetry, art, music and romantic encounters for millions of living species.

ON A DARK CANVAS

There is nothing quite as spectacular as light dancing over the blue-black night sky. A meteor streaks overhead like a heavenly brushstroke. Stars sparkle like diamonds as the Milky Way

Day and night are caused by the rotation of the earth in its orbit around the sun. In the night sky we get a glimpse of the universe that lies beyond earth's atmosphere. MURATART/SHUTTERSTOCK.COM

spreads its wispy veil. In polar skies, the ***aurora borealis*** and ***aurora australis*** shimmer and shine like colorful silk scarves blowing in the wind. Wouldn't life on earth be dull without the spectacular play of light and dark? It's wonderful to think that every minute somewhere on this planet there is a brilliant sunrise. At the same time, somewhere else, there is an equally spectacular color-laden sunset, nature's curtain call announcing the arrival of night.

LIGHT AND LIFE

Our sun, over a million times larger than the earth, sends light and energy to our planet. Through ***photosynthesis***, trees and bacteria use chlorophyll, carbon dioxide (CO_2) and water to store the sun's energy. The plants then become a source of energy for ***herbivores***, plant-eating animals. Hibernation, ***molting*** and reproduction are triggered in these animals by changing periods of light and dark. Other animals have synced their activities to lunar cycles. Though the full moon is 400,000 times dimmer than the sun, it still provides enough light for cheetahs

Far away from the glow of city lights, the night sky becomes rich with stars. The Milky Way, visible in this photo, is a hazy band of over 200 billion stars, all of them in our own galaxy. PERE SANZ/DREAMSTIME.COM

It is a myth that wolves howl more often during a full moon. Though the additional light can make some nocturnal animals more active, others retreat into the shadows for safety.
MARTIN RUEGNER/GETTY IMAGES

DARK MATTERS

Pit vipers can detect infrared light (IR). Heat-sensing pits on the viper's head help locate warm-blooded victims. Humans can't detect IR naturally, but *thermal-imaging cameras* can locate animals (and people) in the dark.

to emerge from hiding to hunt on the African savanna. The full moon, along with acute night vision, helps them track their prey. Wildebeests, gazelles, warthogs and rabbits adapted to daylight are often unable to see the cheetah—until it's too late.

The moon's gravitational pull also controls the ocean tides. In the darkest nights of the lunar cycle in Palau, an island country in the South Pacific, bumphead parrotfish wait for the tide to turn, their faces flushing white with reproductive hormones. When the ocean current starts to pull out, the female parrotfish release their eggs, and the males, sometimes in groups of a thousand or more, rush out and spew plumes of sperm. The outgoing tide sweeps the fertilized eggs farther out into the ocean.

BEYOND PURPLE

The light humans see is only a small part of the total light in the universe. Many animals, insects and birds are able to see a broader range of frequencies than humans can. The ability to see ultraviolet (UV) light has been observed in ants, mice and lizards. UV vision helps bees find patterns in flowers that point toward valuable nectar sources. Kestrels, one of the smallest *raptors*, follow their prey from the sky with the help of UV vision. Rodents like voles, mice and shrews (and dogs, you might have noticed) often mark their territorial journeys with urine. Guess what? Urine reflects UV light. Researchers continue to discover many more organisms that use light signals invisible to humans to survive in the wild. But we have yet to discover how light pollution is affecting them.

LIGHT DETECTIVES

As life evolved on Earth, some animals developed crude light-sensitive cells (photoreceptors) that convert light into electrical signals. About 550 million years ago certain species collected these photoreceptors into a small impression or pit, developing a basic light-sensitive organ. A lens evolved in later animals that served to protect the receptor cells in the head and help focus the light. Animals with the ability to see have become some of the most abundant and successful animals on Earth. Today there are many types of animal eyes custom-designed for where the animal lives and how it behaves. Insect eyes have multiple lenses, arranged to allow them to detect even the smallest movements. The eyes in frogs are oversized to collect as much light as possible in the dark, leaving little room for anything else in their skulls.

The eyes of **vertebrate** animals have two types of photo-receptors, *rods* and *cones*. Animals active in the day have more cones, which function best in bright, colorful environments. However, eyes rich in cones are slower to adapt to changes in light. The eyes of species active at night are often rich in rods, helping them to see better in low light.

A black leopard, one of Africa's most elusive big cats, has eyes that adapt to low-light environments quickly. Its excellent night vision makes the leopard a dangerous predator to encounter. FREDER/GETTY IMAGES

This electromagnetic spectrum shows a range of frequencies, from low (radio waves) to high (gamma radiation), as well as the temperatures they emit. The limited range of human vision is clearly illustrated. VECTOR MINE/SHUTTERSTOCK.COM

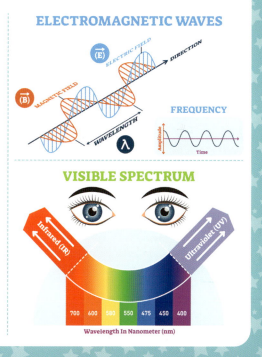

This night view of a Nepalese village on the way up to Everest base camp in the Himalayan mountains shows how artificial lighting has spread into even the remotest areas on Earth. DANIEL PRUDEK/DREAMSTIME.COM

These two red-eyed tree frogs blend in to their Costa Rican environment when they are asleep. But when they are disturbed, brightly colored eyes, legs and feet act as a defense mechanism to confuse and distract predators.
MIRASWONDERLAND/SHUTTERSTOCK.COM

THE ECOLOGY OF NIGHT

Darkness is just as important as light for the survival of living species. *Nocturnal* animals need the cover of darkness to protect themselves from predators when they migrate, look for food, find mates, reproduce and build nests. Species active during the day need the darkness of night for rest to restore their energy reserves. Plants may not be as mobile as animals, but they are very sensitive to changing light conditions. Many of the ways plants behave are triggered by the *photoperiod*, the length of day and night in a 24-hour period. Shorter days and colder temperatures cause plants to drop their leaves in the fall. Longer, warmer days in the spring trigger flowering, pollination and the formation of fruit.

When I first visited the foothills of the Himalayas several decades ago, there were only a few village lights dotting the hillsides. Year after year more lights appeared, and the forests thinned. Now lights cascade into the gullies and forests and up into the sky. The nocturnal animals like leopards, mountain lions and coyotes have climbed higher into the less-populated forests above. Once their retreat reaches the tree line, I fear they will have no place to go.

EYES BUILT FOR THE NIGHT

Almost all amphibians (creatures like frogs and salamanders), half of all *invertebrates* and close to three out of four mammals are nocturnal. That's a lot of nocturnal species! Their eyes have evolved over millions of years to see better in the dark. Owls, for example, have both keen night vision *and* acute hearing. Have you ever noticed how an owl seems to stare and stare? That's because its eyes are so large they can barely move in their sockets. Instead, the pupils widen to collect more light.

The tarsier, a nocturnal primate, has such large, light-capturing eyes that they occupy most of its skull. Members of the cat family and *ungulates,* including deer, cattle and horses have a reflective surface behind the retina, called the tapetum. This layer reflects light that the photoreceptors miss—a second chance to collect more photons of light and see better in low-light conditions.

ADAPTED TO THE DARK

When you can't see in the dark, sounds become very important. Geckos carefully poke their heads out of their hiding places and start chirping in the night to attract potential mates. The aye-aye, a type of lemur, locates its prey by using *echolocation*—it is the only primate known to do so. Other animals rely on smell to find their way through the night. Jacobson's organ, located on the roof of the mouth or in the nasal chamber of many animals, enhances their ability to pick up scents. Many animals use scent markings to communicate and mark territory. Snakes forge forth confident in their sense of taste, flicking their tongues as they slither along the dark ground. Speaking of tongues, Mexican long-tongued bats, avoiding the hot desert sun, feed on cactus flower nectar at night, pollinating them in the process with their siphon-like tongues. Whiskers guide other animals. The hair on spiders' bodies helps them feel their way through the darkness.

CREATURES OF THE LIGHT

One in five mammals are diurnal, more active in the day. They spend their days hunting for food, building nests, and establishing and defending territories (like the robins that nested on our front porch). We humans are diurnal, studying, working, eating, shopping and playing in the day and sleeping at night. Many animals shed thick winter coats in the spring as daylight hours

The Spring Postman

Birds build nests when daylight hours increase in the spring. As darkness decreases, more time is available for mating, nest-building and territorial defense behaviors. Young chicks strengthen their wings and learn to fend for themselves before the long nights and cold weather set in.

When I was four, two robins built a nest over the light on our front porch. The next day when the postal carrier came to deliver the mail, the robins went into full attack mode. Hearing the cries of alarm, my brother and I dashed to the front window to watch the battle. This war went on day after day. Finally, spurred on by the carrier's threats to stop delivering our mail, my dad gently relocated the robins' nest. Years later I learned that robins are protected by the Migratory Bird Treaty Act, and it is illegal to move an active nest. I'll bet the postal carrier didn't know that, and I'm certain he wouldn't have cared.

REIMAR/SHUTTERSTOCK.COM

A Pallas's long-tongued bat drinks nectar from a banana-plant bloom. Nocturnal behavior helps the bats, which are important for seed dispersal and pollination in their tropical environment, avoid predators such as cats and hawks. PETRDD/SHUTTERSTOCK.COM

A brown hare, recognized by its black-tipped ears, is changing between summer and winter coat. The hare's best defense is speed—it can reach speeds of up to 45 mph (72 km/h) while evading predators. PALEKA19/GETTY IMAGES

lengthen and temperatures rise. Others, like rabbits and hares, undergo a change in the color of their fur to blend in with vegetation. When daylight hours shorten, coats turn white to allow animals like the arctic fox to disappear against the winter snow. Some species, like moose and deer, reduce their activities so they consume less energy and therefore need less food. Most important, diurnal animals, no matter at what time of year, still need dark nights to stay safe from predators *and* get well-needed rest.

THE IN-BETWEENERS

Some animals are most active at dawn and twilight. They are known as crepuscular animals and include rabbits, mule deer, elk, moose, bison, ferrets, mice, rats, beavers, river otters, chimney swifts, moths and other insects. You might have noticed that mosquitoes are particularly hungry when the sun is setting.

Animal behavior can vary from one season to the next. Some animals are nocturnal in the summer and diurnal in the winter or even crepuscular when their favorite food is particularly abundant.

Elk are most active at dawn and dusk, choosing to rest during the day. The elk's historical range is shrinking due to agricultural development and lighting from houses and roads spreading into wild areas. FRANKY/DREAMSTIME.COM

One star-filled night at my family's log cabin before we had plumbing, I walked out to the pump after supper with my dog, Amy, to get a bucket of water. A few yards outside the door a large male porcupine was gnawing on some lumber left near the woodshed. He started to move away, but Amy got excited, went in for a sniff and ended up with a dozen porcupine quills stuck in the tip of her nose. Amy braved it out later, sitting perfectly still as I pulled the quills out one by one with a pair of pliers. Ouch! She learned the hard way that porcupines too are crepuscular.

A Malayan porcupine at night. Its quills are used defensively, leaping to attention when the animal is threatened and readily detaching when touched by a predator. Don't stumble onto one of these fellows! TEEKAYU/SHUTTERSTOCK.COM

THE NIGHT MOVERS

Many birds and animals migrate in the relative safety of the night darkness. But how do they find their way? Like all great explorers and voyageurs of the past, they use the night sky as their compass. To study what stars or **constellations** are key guiding lights, some clever researchers used a **planetarium**. They projected stars onto a constructed dome sky. This way they could add and subtract stars in the experiment. Indigo buntings, small seed-eating birds that migrate all over North America, were the subject of one study. They conveniently hop in the direction they are going to fly before they take off. When certain constellations were taken out of the planetarium sky, the buntings lost their sense of direction. This is how the researchers found the key stars that buntings need for their migrations. In another study, a special floating planetarium enabled researchers to identify the stars that guide harbor seals through ocean waters at night.

A young enthusiast with a telescope at sunset. Light pollution has become a problem for amateur astronomers, preventing them from viewing the stars from their backyards. ASTRO STAR/SHUTTERSTOCK.COM

SLEEPING PLANTS

Plants capture energy from sunlight through the process of photosynthesis while absorbing CO_2 from the air and releasing oxygen (O_2), the gas essential for the survival of most living

Nature reserves offer an opportunity to see ecosystems in a relatively natural state. Plants, insects, rodents and other animals form a food chain of energy and nutrients. IMAGE SOURCE/GETTY IMAGES

DARK MATTERS

Mines produce explosive gases that are easily sparked by heat. In the deep dark mines of 19th-century Europe, dried fish skins on the walls provided a safe form of dim lighting. In other countries, miners used fireflies in bottles.

organisms on Earth. Plants directly store the energy of the sun. That's why they're called primary producers. Herbivores eat the plants for energy. Carnivores (meat-eaters) eat the herbivores, and the energy exchange goes on. But plants don't depend only on the sun for survival—they need the dark too! As any good gardener knows, plants need time to replenish their energy reserves. Without regular periods of darkness, plant development is affected, and along with it, the balance of the entire ecosystem. The plants don't grow well, leading to possible food shortages for herbivores. Less food means fewer herbivores and less food for the carnivores. You get the picture. This relationship between plants and animals and the day-night cycle has evolved over billions of years.

THE LIGHT BEARERS

Have you ever walked through the woods at night, the air sparkling with the flash of fireflies? Have you ever watched from the seashore as breaking waves glittered like diamonds? Some of the most magical moments on Earth are created by **bioluminescent** animals and plants, those that make their own light. But why would organisms invest so much of their precious energy into becoming living light boxes when sunlight is available every day? Well, it turns out there are a lot of reasons. The luminous chemical reactions in the abdomens, or "lanterns," of fireflies that make them light up are actually mating signals for potential partners. The flashes double as a warning to rivals to stay away. In some species all the male fireflies flash at the same time, a behavior thought to increase their attractiveness to females, like a natural disco light. Many frogs, marine animals and even mushrooms absorb light and release it later at a different wavelength, causing them to glow at night, a process known as **biofluorescence.**

Glowing fireflies create magical moments in natural environments. They also play a valuable role in ecosystems, feeding on soft-bodied organisms like snails, slugs and mites. TDUB303/GETTY IMAGES

UNDERWATER LIGHTING

Out in deep ocean waters, glowing marine organisms are often the only source of light. Three out of every four sea creatures glow in the dark—jellyfish, squid, flashlight fish, ribbon worms, small crustaceans and even clams. Some species use this "superpower" as a warning to predators. Others use the attraction of light to get mates, while a few, like the anglerfish, use it to lure prey.

But why make light when you can borrow it from others? The Hawaiian bobtail squid is a crafty creature that stores bioluminescent bacteria in a cavity on its underside. The light reduces its dark silhouette against a moonlit sky when viewed from below. This means predators like sharks have difficulty seeing it. Even the tiniest of marine organisms join in the light show. ***Dinoflagellates***, a type of phytoplankton, light up when a hand or paddle moves through the surface of tropical waters, creating what is known as "sea sparkles."

With so many animals having adapted to the dark-light cycle of a spinning Earth, it is no surprise that lights introduced by people are damaging sensitive ecosystems, both on land and underwater.

Jellyfish use their bioluminescent powers to defend themselves. Comb jellies startle predators with bright flashes. They can also release thousands of glowing particles into the water to confuse attackers while they make their escape. TAKESHI SASANUMA/GETTY IMAGES

CHAPTER TWO

Artificial Lights on Land

FROM FIRE TO LIGHT BULBS

Humans have been lighting the night since they learned to control fire a million years ago. Later, ice-age humans made stone lamps that burned animal fat to light their caves. The Romans created beeswax candles that burned so steadily that time could be measured in candle units. But it was Edison's light bulb, invented 150 years ago, that sliced into the darkness of night like never before. Today satellite images show how dramatically night on Earth has changed since then. Lights illuminate the cities, villages and roadways of wealthy nations. The glow from the lights of Los Angeles can be seen in the night sky from as far away as 90 miles (145 kilometers). Light is slowly creeping into wild places at night all over the planet.

Earthenware oil lamps are still used today but largely for rituals and religious ceremonies. The most common oil used in the ancient Mediterranean region was olive oil. Wicks were made of linen or papyrus.
CRISTINA-RAMIREZ/SHUTTERSTOCK.COM

THE DARK TRUTH ABOUT LIGHT

Photons of light do not seem very dangerous when compared with pollutants like toxic chemicals, oil spills or noxious gases. Animals and plants need clean air, soil and water, but life cycles

also need darkness. And around the world, cities that don't sleep are the fastest-growing habitat on Earth. The total area occupied by cities is expected to double over the next three decades. Almost a quarter of the earth's land is now exposed to artificial light at night.

Brightly lit office buildings may have a certain charm at night; however, they add to excess CO_2 in the atmosphere. They also contribute to skyglow that prevents city dwellers from viewing the night sky.
CREATIVE LAB/SHUTTERSTOCK.COM

ENDANGERED NIGHT SKIES

One by one the stars, constellations and even the Milky Way are fading from sight for urban dwellers. Future generations may never get the chance to feel the awe of looking up at the sparkling night sky, knowing that they are looking at galaxies billions of **light-years** away. Observatories are being closed and their telescopes moved to remote places to avoid skyglow from cities. One amateur astronomer, John Bortle, created the nine-level Bortle Scale that measures the relative darkness of the night sky. Class 1 is a naturally dark sky, while class 9 corresponds to a pale inner-city sky. Streetlights, ATM machines, billboards, commercial buildings, security lights, business signs and house lights are all stealing the night from city dwellers. And wild creatures are caught in the glow.

DARK MATTERS

Almost everyone in the United States and Europe is exposed to some light pollution. Four out of five North Americans can't even see the Milky Way when they look up at night.

This wide-angle view shows a panorama of urban lighting. In the United States and Europe, a majority of the public never experiences a natural night sky. JOHANNES SPAHN/GETTY IMAGES

Skyglow above this small town spreads out over the surrounding desert environment. Many desert animals are nocturnal due to extremely high daytime temperatures. TAKA_D/SHUTTERSTOCK.COM

IN TERMS OF LIGHT

Artificial lights can cause difficulties for both people and ecosystems. Here are the main problems and the terms used to describe them.

1. *Glare* is light directed in the wrong way. We've all been blinded by the bright lights of an oncoming vehicle. It's a problem for drivers, but it can also blind animals in their habitats. Glare is caused by overly bright, unshielded light, not just from vehicles but from outdoor lighting fixtures as well.

2. *Clutter* is a type of glare caused by too many lighting fixtures in one place, like rows of bright lights over billboards and large signs.

3. *Light trespass* is light that spills into unintended areas, like streetlights spilling into your house or lit roadways sending light into wild areas. It's caused by using lights that are too bright and by poorly directed light fixtures.

4. *Skyglow* is the result of too many unshielded city lights, especially those that shine upward. The glow can often be seen from hundreds of miles away, and it prevents a proper view of the dark night sky. Around cities with cloudy weather, like Seattle and London, the cloud cover reflects the city lights back to the earth, making the problem worse.

LIGHT POLLUTION

Light is an unusual pollutant. It attracts some animals and repels others. Some bats avoid introduced lights in their natural habitats. As a result, their total feeding area becomes smaller. With fewer pollinating bats, insect populations will increase in size, reducing available vegetation. Other bats take advantage of insects attracted to lights and feed on them. Amphibians like frogs and toads, already under stress from the loss of their

Neon lights and illuminated billboards in Tokyo reflect off rainy streets, illustrating the degree of glare and clutter in an urban environment. NATALIYA HORA/DREAMSTIME.COM

wetland homes, are very sensitive to lights. Studies show that the introduction of bright lights quickly silences the mating calls of male tree frogs.

A cloudy night sky near a city today can be thousands of times brighter than it was two centuries ago. This is one of the most dramatic changes human beings have made to the environment. A recent study shows that in the midwestern United States, the balance between cougars and their prey, mule deer, is increasingly affected by the spread of artificial lights. The mule deer are attracted to the vegetation in lit areas, but it is an ecological trap! Cougars lurk in the dark corners just away from the light, waiting to make their kill.

Over-illuminated buildings at night are a magnet for migrating birds, attracting them from far and wide. Once inside the maze of city buildings, many birds have difficulty escaping. DAVE ROBERTS/DREAMSTIME.COM

A cougar roams the night with the lights of Los Angeles in the background. Cougars mostly hunt at dawn and dusk, but near populated areas they will hunt at night to avoid contact with people. JOHANNA TURNER

Collisions with windows can occur in the day or night. Birds do not recognize daytime reflections in windows—they don't see glass as a solid barrier until they strike it.
LUCIA HISATSUGA/GETTY IMAGES

⭐⭐ DARK MATTERS

An estimated 300 million to 1 billion birds die every year in North America by colliding with buildings—7 million from collisions with communication towers alone. Many of these birds are on their migrations.

THE HIGH-RISE AND THE MIGRATOR

Many birds migrate at night, when there are fewer predators and winds settle down. Lights are a big threat to migrant bird populations. Brightly lit high-rise buildings can attract huge flocks of migrators, especially when the night sky is hidden by clouds and skyglow is brightest. Many mass deaths have occurred when flocks collided with buildings and other lit structures. Young birds in particular are easily confused by the maze of lights in the city at night.

Birds are attracted to light in natural ecosystems as well. Sound-recording experiments from the University of Windsor show that three times as many migratory bird calls are heard in wild areas with artificial lights as there are in unlit areas. The birds are essentially "captured" by the lights, especially on nights with low-lying clouds when the migrators cannot see the moon and stars. A flight-path diversion can delay a bird's arrival at breeding or wintering grounds or can even shorten its life span.

Some cities, like Toronto and New York, are located on the paths of hundreds of migrating bird species. During peak migration season, tens of thousands of birds pass over Toronto in a single hour. The tiny blackpoll warbler is among them, on its

A wedge of geese flies over Calgary at sunrise. More than half of the building surfaces in modern cities are made of glass. Since 1970, bird populations in Canada and the United States have shrunk by about three billion birds. LISA BOURGEAULT/DREAMSTIME.COM

5,000-mile (8,000-kilometer) journey from South America to Alaska. At every stop along their migratory route, the birds arrive with little or no fat reserves left on their bodies. Rooftop terraces can be attractive roosts for the birds, but when they launch they are confronted with a confusion of reflective glass. Shutters and awnings over the windows of lit buildings have proven effective in reducing the light spilling out into flight paths. Important organizations like the Canadian charity Fatal Light Awareness Program (FLAP) teach building owners and others about the dangers that lit building structures present to birds in flight. For the past 30 years they have helped research and develop solutions to this ongoing problem in cities.

Decals have been applied to the windows of this warehouse in Brisbane, Australia. Studies show that decals and other window coverings can reduce bird deaths. VINEYARD PERSPECTIVE/SHUTTERSTOCK.COM

THE EARLY BIRD AND THE WORM

The morning and evening choruses of songbirds are triggered by the arrival and the disappearance of light. Studies show that light pollution causes many bird species to start singing earlier in the morning and extend their evening chorus later into the night. There are reports of some species, confused by artificial lights, singing throughout the night. Light at night can also affect the seasonal behavior of some birds, causing them to reproduce later in the fall. Rapidly declining temperatures and dwindling food sources can be fatal for fragile chicks. Some species nesting near lights start to breed too early in the spring, once again threatening the survival of young chicks. Unfortunately, when it comes to light pollution the early bird does not always get the worm.

A lot of urban lighting is unshielded. This can lead to over-illumination and glare, creating visibility problems for both people and wildlife. ENOLABRAIN/GETTY IMAGES

SPOTLIGHT ON INSECTS

Summer nights on the porch with family and friends...who doesn't love it? Of course, it would be nicer without the bugs, especially pesky moths circling the lights and dropping down

Insects swarm an ornate streetlamp. Studies indicate an alarming loss of insect populations due to street and porch lighting. This leads to a disruption of the food chain and a "vacuum cleaner" effect on protein in the ecosystem. PECHEVOY/GETTY IMAGES

into drinks and snacks. *Phototaxis* is a term used to describe the movement of insects in response to the introduction of light. Moths are active at night, but they are attracted to light. For millions of years the sun and moon have acted as guiding lights for insects. But artificial lights emit in all directions, so insects cannot keep them at the same angle to their flight paths as they would with the celestial signposts. This creates a trap, causing the insect to fly in circles. Light-trapped insects eventually run out of energy and die, removing a valuable protein source for bats, birds and frogs. Lights can also act as a wall, or "crash barrier," limiting an insect's habitat range.

Male fireflies light up their abdomens hoping for a response from potential mates. Porch lights, streetlights and car headlights are now competing with their flashy behavior.

MAMMALS OF THE NIGHT

A young girl befriends a wallaby joey (baby) in Australia. Light pollution can put young marsupials at risk of missing seasonal food sources, hindering their development. CHAMELEONSEYE/GETTY IMAGES

Lights expose nocturnal mammals to the lurking eyes of predators, making them hesitant to feed and mate. Their eyes, rich in rods, quickly become saturated by exposure to bright lights, causing temporary blindness. Many mammals die at night because of collisions with vehicles. Over 29 million mammals are killed this way every year in Europe, and most of those deaths occur between dusk and dawn.

Artificial lights streaming into ecosystems can disrupt biological clocks. Melatonin, a hormone that regulates sleep patterns and reproductive activity in mammals, needs darkness for release. Lights at night can lower melatonin levels in mammals. Wallabies are marsupials, mammals that carry their young in pouches like kangaroos do. Studies show that their reproductive cycles are thrown off by artificial lights. The birth of their offspring can be delayed by as much as a month, reducing the size of adults and disrupting their ability to hibernate.

BATS IN CAULDRONS

Almost all *insectivorous* bats feed at night, when there are lots of insects. Creatures of habit, bats use routine "commuter routes" when heading to feeding areas. Rows of streetlights create walls of light that bats are hesitant to cross in case predators are lurking nearby. And lights that invade the dark roosts of hibernating bats can break their *dormant state*, endangering their ability to survive the cold season. Bright lights also blind the light-sensitive eyes of bats and can delay the departure of the cauldron (colony of bats) from the roost. This means less time for eating, potentially threatening the survival of the cauldron and upsetting ecosystem balance.

Not all bats avoid light. You might even see bats circling streetlights at night, feeding at the all-you-can-eat bugfest. Brown bats have been known to eat up to 1,200 insects an hour.

A cauldron of bats emerges at sunset to start its night of feeding. Even a little lighting can affect brown-bat habitats and impact the insect-population management these species provide. PHOTOONGRAPHY/SHUTTERSTOCK.COM

FROGS ON BLIND DATES

Amphibians like frogs, toads and salamanders gobble up their fair share of bugs too—mostly at night. Many amphibians are naturally fluorescent and glow green under certain wavelengths of light. One streetlamp is 500 times brighter than the moon, and it makes amphibians more visible to predators such as hawks. The headlights of a passing vehicle can be up to 10,000 times brighter, temporarily blinding amphibian eyes. This prevents them from catching fast-moving insects or getting off the road to avoid a fatal collision.

Studies show that amphibian life stages are affected by light pollution, possibly lowering growth rates in juvenile American toads. Male green frogs were shown to produce fewer mating calls, making them less attractive to the females that select mates by their calls. Lower melatonin levels reduce frogs' ability to change color to blend into the environment and to adjust to temperature changes.

Studies show that American toad fatalities increase on roads with artificial lighting. Amphibians are typically attracted to lights, with some variation between species. TANYA MAY/SHUTTERSTOCK.COM

PLANTS AND TREES

Plants rely on the photoperiod to know when seasons are changing. You might think that photosynthetic organisms like plants would benefit from more light at night. But no, artificial lights are typically below the brightness threshold for photosynthesis. They encourage plants to produce larger leaves with more pores that stay open longer. But that just makes them more vulnerable to pollution and drought, common problems in the city environment.

A New York City study showed that leaf fall can be delayed by as much as a month because of urban lighting. Trees that keep their leaves longer are more likely to suffer ice damage, especially if the cold weather comes early. Trees growing near lights also tend to flower earlier in the spring, which again increases the risk of frost damage.

IN A HEALTHY LIGHT

Eighty percent of the world's population lives under skyglow at night. What effect is it having on human health? The cells that detect light in our eyes are very sensitive. They send signals to our brains that start a lot of different *physiological* processes. Take melatonin for instance. In humans, as in other mammals, melatonin secretion is reduced when an organism is exposed to lights at night. A lack of melatonin can increase the risk of mood swings and anxiety, especially in children.

Do you know that you have a clock in your body? The *circadian clock* is a 24-hour "timepiece" that regulates sleep, activity patterns and hunger, but it is disrupted by light at night. Light-emitting diodes, better known as LEDs, have dramatically reduced energy consumption for lighting. But they have a downside. LEDs emit light at wavelengths in the blue range of the visible spectra.

Most modern cities now function 24 hours a day, and lights are required for most human activity. But what are our electronic devices and streetlights doing to our health? URBAZON/GETTY IMAGES

Blue light suppresses the secretion of melatonin even more than the yellow-spectrum light of traditional incandescent light bulbs. Many experts are calling for a limit on smartphones, tablets and computers at night. That's why you may see some devices now with software to warm the light emitted at night.

Researchers are exploring the links between night lighting and chronic diseases, particularly cancer and obesity. Do you look at your cell phone, tablet or computer screen in your room at night? If you do, have you ever considered what it is doing to your health? Screen time during the COVID-19 pandemic reportedly increased with so many people restricted to indoor activities. Try *not* looking at a screen at night for a full week. Does it make a difference to your sleep cycle? Do you sleep more deeply or for a longer period?

It would be easy to conclude that light pollution is only a problem on land, where most human activity takes place. However, marine and freshwater environments are particularly sensitive to light since it readily passes through the surface layers of water. Skyglow from cities and the lights of fishing vessels, oil rigs and icebreakers are disrupting ocean ecosystems, from coastal seabeds to vulnerable coral reefs.

A young face bathed in the blue light from an LED screen has become a commonplace sight over the last decade or so. More medical research is needed to determine blue light's effects on human health and development. KIRIILL RYZHOV/DREAMSTIME.COM

Night Workers

When I was in high school, my friends and I worked the night shift at the post office over the winter holidays. Extra help was needed at a time when cards and gifts overwhelmed post office employees. It was strange to stay up all night and come home when the sun was rising. It is only now that I realize the potential effects of the night shift on human health. Several recent studies show that working this shift for a long time (a period of four years or more) can lead to an increase in cancer, particularly breast cancer in women. Melatonin plays a role in stopping the growth of tumors, and lack of darkness suppresses melatonin output. The International Agency for Research on Cancer concludes that shift work is probably **carcinogenic**.

In cities that never sleep, the dividing line between night and day has become increasingly blurred. Many businesses specialize in catering to people who are active at night, offering their food and products 24 hours a day.
MICKEYTEAM/SHUTTERSTOCK.COM

CHAPTER THREE

Lighting the Oceans, Lakes and Rivers

THE ECOLOGY OF THE NIGHT SEA

Marine ecosystems are structured very differently from those on land. Light reaches the surface layers of the water, the *photic zone*, where the photosynthetic organisms like phytoplankton, algae and other marine plants live. These organisms provide food and energy for those living in the dark waters below 250 feet (80 meters). Photosynthesis in the ocean absorbs carbon dioxide from the air and provides a full half of all the earth's atmospheric oxygen. At night zooplankton rise up to feed on surface phytoplankton. Tiny fish larvae, bristle-mouths, squid and giant baleen whales ascend to feed on the smaller organisms above. This grand vertical migration ends at dawn, when predators descend back into the ocean depths.

Skyglow from cities often extends hundreds of miles out to sea. Three out of four of the world's largest cities are situated on the coast. Coastal lights also spread out along the shallow seabed near land. Seabed-dwelling organisms like sea squirts and bristle worms are reportedly moving away from lit coastal seafloors. Salmon are also changing their behavior around brightly lit coasts. Juvenile salmon feed and migrate near the shore to avoid ocean predators. Many are attracted to the coastal lights, but studies show that their predators have discovered this attraction and are now using lit coasts as feeding zones, threatening salmon populations.

Clownfish swim by a bubble tip anemone in this coral reef. Typically found in shallow coastal waters, coral reefs are increasingly vulnerable to light spilling over from coastal development. MARTA_KENT/GETTY IMAGES

ON THE BEACH

Females of all seven species of sea turtles migrate thousands of miles to lay their eggs on the very beaches where they were born. Crawling out of dark waters, they lay their eggs in the sand under the cover of night and then return to the sea. Tiny hatchlings soon emerge, quickly heading seaward. How do they know which way to go?

Recent research shows that the young sea turtles are guided by the darkness of the beach, not by the lure of glittering ocean waters as previously thought. Beachfront lighting disorients hatchlings, leaving them vulnerable to predators like hawks and gulls. Many wander onto roadways, confused by streetlights, vehicles, billboards and illuminated buildings and homes, only to be crushed by passing vehicles. Beachfront cleanups that remove dune vegetation like sedges and grasses only add to the problem. Plants act as a natural shield from lights and reflective surfaces for the turtle nests.

CORAL REEFS AT NIGHT

Coral reefs come alive in the light—both sunlight *and* moonlight. Sponges, sea anemones, flatworms, clownfish, parrotfish, scorpionfish, sea stars, sea cucumbers, squid, snails, sharks and rays all feed at the coral-reef restaurant. Tiny algae called *zooxanthellae*, in a **symbiotic** relationship with the corals, provide oxygen and

These freshly hatched sea turtles in Costa Rica are having no trouble deciding the way to the ocean. Some frantic swimming and an undertow will take them out into safer waters, but only one in a thousand will survive. SUSAN M JACKSON/SHUTTERSTOCK.COM

DARK MATTERS

Warm-colored yellow or red light bulbs in shielded light fixtures are more friendly for sea turtles. This light directed toward the ground is less disturbing to emerging hatchlings seeking their ocean home.

Acropora corals spawn once a year, given proper day length, tide height and water temperature. They release their tiny egg and sperm bundles during the full-moon phase of the lunar cycle. CORAL BRUNNER/SHUTTERSTOCK.COM

food in exchange for shelter. Studies show that the rhythms of the moon play an important role in the health of coral reefs. But coastal lights are now interfering with the ability of the corals to detect moonlight. The algae that live inside the corals decline in number in the presence of lights at night. Conservationists are concerned that skyglow and coastal lighting will adversely affect the life cycle of other reef animals too. Not a single hatchling survived in an experiment on reef-dwelling clownfish eggs exposed to low levels of light.

Lighthouses, built to assist human ocean navigation, can cause mass bird fatalities, particularly under cloudy conditions. One interesting study, however, found that fewer migrating seabirds were attracted to blinking lights than to a constant spotlight. 9PARUSNIKOV/DREAMSTIME.COM

MARINE BIRDS

Have you ever seen a lighthouse with its sweeping spotlights warning ocean vessels that they are approaching the rocky coastline? Oil rigs and fishing boats are also highly illuminated. These things all attract huge numbers of fish *and* marine birds. Many mass deaths have occurred from birds flying into the brightly

Dimming Coastal Lights

A study started by a 16-year-old boy named Zachary Weishampel, whose father is a biology professor in Florida, looked at annual records and satellite images of coastal lighting from 1992 to 2012. During this period Florida beaches became darker at night, despite the population having increased by more than five million people. That's because lighting regulations by municipal authorities set cutoff times for coastal lights and added shielded light fixtures with longer-wavelength (warm yellow) light bulbs. Zachary, his father and a graduate student found that the number of nesting females had increased in almost 250 sea-turtle sites. Other beach organisms benefited as well. This research shows that lighting changes work!

Scientists are studying the effects of light pollution on crabs, barnacles and mussels on coastal seabeds. A new international collaboration called the Global Artificial Light Ocean Network (GLOW) is investigating the effects of light pollution on coastal algae and invertebrates.

Drivers in Fort Lauderdale, FL, are warned that street lights will not be turned on at night to assist hatchlings trying to find their way back to ocean waters.
SERENETHOS / DREAMSTIME.COM

lit structures. Most of these collisions occurred in bad weather, under a new moon or during peak migration periods. A few years ago a research boat using powerful lights to detect icebergs was struck by close to a thousand seabirds, killing over 200 of them. In another incident during bad weather, close to 6,000 birds landed on the deck of a brightly lit fishing vessel. Altogether they weighed over a ton—they almost sank the ship.

Flames flare up to 65 feet (20 meters) in the air on oil-drilling platforms, burning off excess gas. Seabirds expect to find food when they see light since many feed on bioluminescent organisms like squid. Attracted to the flares, many birds fly straight at them, incinerating themselves in the process. Others circle the light like moths, eventually dropping exhausted into the oily waters below. Commercial fishers also use bright lights, attempting to attract fish and squid to the surface. Marine birds often get hooked on the fishing lines. Coastal lights are a further threat, disturbing the nesting sites of marine birds like petrels and shearwaters.

A large offshore oil rig lights up an entire coastal area at night. Light pollution can disrupt the circadian rhythm of marine life, affecting reproduction, migration and feeding. NUM_SKYMAN/SHUTTERSTOCK.COM

'CUSTOM-EYES-ED' SEABIRDS

Have you ever spent a day at the beach and come back with your eyes all red and sunburned? That's due to the high level of UV light reflected from the sand and water. So how do seabirds manage to protect their eyes on their long-distance migrations? Scientists theorize that droplets of oil found in the birds' eyes screen out UV light—just like a pair of UV-protection sunglasses.

Marine birds that dive for food need to see both in the air and under water. When Australasian gannets hit the water on a high-speed dive, the shape of their lenses quickly changes, enabling them to immediately focus on underwater objects. Penguins also adapt their lenses underwater, using their strong eye muscles. They also have a membranous third eyelid to protect them from debris underwater.

Keen eyesight helps this Bulwer's petrel spot its favorite food in the waters below. These seabirds feed on tiny crustaceans called krill. VICTOR SUAREZ NARANJO/SHUTTERSTOCK.COM

In tropical coastal regions you may find bioluminescent plankton glowing under the warm surface waters at night. Grab a magnifying glass, and you can see thousands of these tiny microorganisms in a single drop of water.
JAMES_STONE76/SHUTTERSTOCK.COM

A LANTERN, A SEAL AND THE RED DEVIL

So what do you do all day long when you live in deep, dark ocean waters, waiting for your chance to rise at night? You create your own light, that's what! Three out of four marine organisms in the deep are bioluminescent. The hundreds of different species of lanternfish got their common name because of their ability to produce light as if carrying their own lanterns. The light comes from tiny **photophores** on their heads, undersides and tails, attracting smaller prey like a shiny fisher's lure. Their big eyes help them find and feed on zooplankton, the popcorn of the sea and a popular midnight snack for many marine animals.

The giant Humboldt squid, known as the Red Devil, turns bright red when it's disturbed. Color cells in surface tissue are backlit by photophores in the muscle below, allowing the squid to glow in color. Scientists believe that the squid communicate using these light shows while hunting for prey. Light pollution on surface waters could affect this unique communication system.

FRESHWATER ECOSYSTEMS

Artificial lights also invade lakes, ponds and rivers, disrupting freshwater ecosystems. Lakes close to city centers are most at risk because their water is clearer and transmits light more readily. Lakes in rural areas near wetlands are cloudy with organic particles, which lowers their light transmission. Spawning perch are affected by light while they're on their journeys to lay eggs. At night many

The photophores of a firefly squid produce a pattern of glowing blue spots. Every spring in Japan large numbers of this species gather to spawn, illuminating entire beaches and attracting tourists from all over the world. RONGUI/GETTY IMAGES

With a small net you can see many organisms living and reproducing in mountain streams, from fish to amphibians and insects in various stages of their life cycles.
WUNDERVISUALS/GETTY IMAGES

freshwater fish produce melatonin, important for their development. Even low levels of light at night can suppress its release.

Darkness triggers certain behaviors in aquatic insects, particularly those who spend part of their life cycle in rivers and streams, known as riparian ecosystems. Mayfly nymphs and blackfly larvae develop in moving water. At night they detach from their perches on reeds and rocks and float downstream in the water column—a behavior called *stream drift*. They stay attached during full-moon periods, when the larvae would be more exposed to predators. In polar regions, the increase in light during the summer can eliminate drift altogether. Night lighting results in the larvae and nymphs staying attached to the fixed surfaces, reducing their habitat range. Light is an important part of freshwater ecosystems just as it is in the oceans.

DAZZLED BY THE LIGHT

Shiny objects reflect light. They do this by collecting scattered light waves on their surfaces and redirecting them as **polarized light**. Light reflects off the surface of water in much the same way. Have you ever noticed dragonflies landing on shiny objects during the summer? They are looking for water, which is where they lay their eggs, and where the nymphs develop until they emerge as adults and fly away. Reflections from shiny surfaces confuse as many as 300 different aquatic insects, threatening their populations and the animals that depend on them.

Scientists are starting to realize that polarized light provides a messaging system in the animal kingdom that guides behavior. For example, some studies show that polarized light, like UV light, may be used by flowers to attract pollinators. Another report indicates that plant viruses may change the polarized light on leaf surfaces to attract prey they can feed upon.

Light introduced into the natural environment can become a serious pollutant. Let's take a look at what is being done about it. The world has some brave knights defending the darkness. You too can become a guardian of the night!

DARK MATTERS

Tiny single-celled dinoflagellates create a twinkling seascape known as the Blue Tears of China. But they feed on toxic algae, making them poisonous to others, including people.

A dragonfly sits on an outdoor light. Most insects are attracted to light, resulting in light pollution becoming a major cause of insect-population declines.
ANGIE AMIL/DREAMSTIME.COM

CHAPTER FOUR

Guardians of the Night

Switching from incandescent bulbs to LED lights can save energy and money. Warm-colored bulbs (yellow) are preferable. However, shutting off exterior lights of any kind at night is the most effective way to prevent the loss of insect pollinators.
JARI HINDSTROEM/SHUTTERSTOCK.COM

DEFENDERS OF DARKNESS

We can reduce unwanted or misdirected light in our daily lives. Light is the one form of pollution that can be reduced immediately by flipping a switch.

Many of us have seen the "blue marble" photos of Earth taken by NASA satellites. Our planet looks delicate and vulnerable—because it is. More recently NASA released "black marble" photographs, powerful images of the earth at night. They show how much darkness has been lost on our planet from artificial lighting over time. But the good news is that we can help—one porch light, one streetlight, one building, one community at a time. Switch off lights that have no purpose. Shield light fixtures so the light goes where it's needed. Switch light bulbs to warmer colors (red and yellow). We have to remove the extra stress of light pollution on threatened plant and animal habitats.

Our planet no longer sleeps. Just over a hundred years ago, none of the lights in this photograph were visible from space. Darkness is an endangered commodity—even though it is essential to the survival of living species. BLUE PLANET STUDIO/SHUTTERSTOCK.COM

CARBON EMISSIONS AND WASTED LIGHT

Light pollution is a worldwide problem. Measurements from around the globe are needed to study the effects of artificial lights. That's where **citizen science** comes in. You can help by participating in Globe at Night, a campaign that collects measurements of night-sky brightness. Sky-brightness data from close to 30,000 locations in 2020 alone helped measure light pollution around the world.

Globe at Night's Adopt-a-Street Program is a campaign that anyone can get involved with, young or old. Consider helping coordinate people to provide brightness measurements at every mile of major roadway near you. This data can then be used for research on the effect of streetlighting on wildlife and human health.

The sparkling night sky that inspired artists like Vincent van Gogh and writers like William Shakespeare is being lost to new generations of youth. A starless sky due to skyglow is all that is seen here in Brisbane, Australia. NEIL GAVIN/GETTY IMAGES

LED streetlights illuminate this stretch of road, spilling over into the trees and fields nearby. Reducing their strength and shielding the lights can help reduce the harsh glare experienced by drivers and the disruption of nearby ecosystems. MILAN NOGA/SHUTTERSTOCK.COM

ENERGY $AVINGS

Too much lighting wastes valuable energy, especially when it spills into areas where it is not needed. Over 90 percent of outdoor lighting in the United States illuminates roadways and parking lots. A full third of that light is wasted. In the province of Quebec alone, the estimated annual cost to taxpayers of mis-directed or wasted light is $50 million. Immediate savings can be made by using timers and installing motion-detector lights for outside security. Indoor lighting can also be reduced by shutting lights off in empty rooms at home and in empty office buildings.

LEDs use up to 90 percent less energy and last up to 25 times longer than traditional light bulbs, helping reduce energy costs further—but beware of the blues. LEDs that emit blue light affect the biological clock of many living organisms. When possible, choose warm-white bulbs to minimize the impact on yourself and others. More than 8 percent of all energy use in the United States

Surfside Success

Bright lights on the exterior of the Kauai Surf Hotel in Hawaii were responsible for almost half of Hawaiian seabird groundings (when birds are forced to land) in 1981. Conservationists were shocked, and lighting experts were brought in. Lights were reduced in brightness and fixtures were shielded, preventing them from shining up into the sky, out into the ocean and into surrounding areas. Special measures were taken to reduce skyward lighting during periods when *fledglings* were first venturing out into ocean waters. The changes worked. The County of Kauai started a program to insulate and shield streetlights that has reduced the number of grounded shearwaters and petrels even further.

Shearwaters travel hundreds of thousands of miles in their lifetime. Their figure-eight journey from the Arctic to the Antarctic takes them to each pole at its respective summer months, when seafood is abundant. Lighting guidelines are needed to protect the migratory routes of marine birds that cross international borders.

The unique topography of the Nā Pali coast of Kauai harbors a rich diversity of flora and fauna. Every new development needs its own lighting guidelines to reduce disruption to local ecosystems. IGNACIO PALACIOS/GETTY IMAGES

is for lighting, most of that to light the night. Can you imagine how much could be saved by switching bulbs to LEDs?

Total energy use in the United States has not changed in more than 20 years due to some of the energy-saving measures just mentioned, even though the economy has grown 30 percent. But there is so much more efficiency that can be achieved. Successful lighting laws in Kennebunkport, Maine, and Tucson, Arizona, are models for other municipalities. Successful lighting regulations reduce glare, energy usage, light trespass and financial costs to communities. Some cities, like Eatontown, New Jersey, have combined regulations regarding noise and glare into a single ordinance.

LIGHTING FOR SAFETY

Many people believe that more lighting means more security. But overlighting can be counterproductive. When light is too bright, it causes glare, reducing one's ability to see into shadows. The solution is not *more* lighting but *effective* lighting. Light sources should not be visible from the property line, and they should be directed downward to avoid shining directly into people's eyes. Security lighting is most effective when it is motion activated. When motion-activated security lights are used, neighbors are more alert to light coming from next door at night.

A study in West Essex, UK, showed that crime actually increased in lit areas. Though residents believed that more lighting would reduce crime, the installation of all-night lights resulted in a 55 percent increase in criminal activity. Police reports indicate that dark areas are often safer than areas that are lit. In the United States, a "dark campus" policy started in San Antonio resulted in a decrease in vandalism. Incidences of graffiti were also reduced when all-night exterior lights were shut off. Have you ever tried to draw in the dark? It's hard to be proud of your work when the lights come back on.

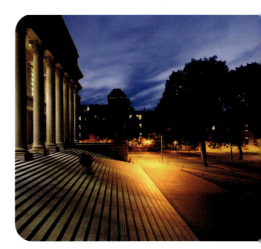

Students gather on the steps of a building on the Harvard University campus. Shielded lights with warm-colored bulbs can make for a more pleasing and safer experience for people out at night. JORGEANTONIO/GETTY IMAGES

Far from the city lights, an adult and a young enthusiast with binoculars enjoy identifying the constellations and celestial bodies in the night sky. VCHAL/SHUTTERSTOCK.COM

KEEPING AN EYE OUT FOR THE NIGHT

Conservation planning has been slow to wake up to the impacts of artificial lighting. As deforestation, climate change, and water, soil and air pollution have captured the limelight, light pollution has stood quietly nearby in the shadows. But it can no longer be ignored.

Conservationists must track night-lighting research and add it to their planning efforts to save species and habitats. For example, nocturnal mammals are hesitant to enter **wildlife corridors** that are lit or close to brightly lit areas. Animal-corridor designs and their locations in ecosystems need to take into account the amount of lighting animals will tolerate without leaving the corridor. When looking at the impact of new projects such as buildings, bridges, mining operations and quarries, lighting information needs to be included to assess its effect on the night environment.

Large nocturnal mammals have broad ranges that are often divided by roads. Wildlife corridors like this one are active at night, but more studies are needed to determine the best lighting conditions to encourage animals to cross safely. FONTI.PL/SHUTTERSTOCK.COM

DARK SKIES

The International Dark-Sky Association (IDA) has established guidelines to reduce skyglow and minimize the effects of light spreading into surrounding ecosystems. Pale night skies due to skyglow from cities make it difficult for both amateur and professional astronomers to study the stars. The IDA has certified dark-sky preserves and national parks with established lighting rules. "Astrotourism" is rapidly growing in popularity. There are more than 60 dark-sky places in the United States alone. Have you ever looked through a high-powered telescope into a star-studded night sky? If you haven't, you should! It's like being transported out into the galaxy.

At least 19 states in the United States have laws to limit light pollution, promoting energy conservation, public safety and astronomical research. In Ann Arbor, Michigan, lighting regulations

DARK MATTERS

As of August 2021 there were 180 certified dark-sky places around the world. They are sprinkled across Canada from Bon Accord in Alberta to Quetico Provincial Park in Ontario to Mont-Mégantic in Quebec.

Sometimes the biggest decision regarding new lights is when to shut them off.
FADHEIT/GETTY IMAGES

Shutting off lights when leaving a room is a good habit to cultivate. If outside lights are not on a timer or motion detector, consider shutting those off late at night too. The local wildlife and plants will appreciate it.
DMYTRO VIETROV/SHUTTERSTOCK.COM

Shielded wall lights that are directed downward are most effective. Light spilling upward contributes to artificial skyglow. ANTON BELO/SHUTTERSTOCK.COM

were enacted "to enhance the quality of life." Some municipal governments have placed lighting regulations directly in their zoning codes.

WHAT CAN YOU DO?

When installing new exterior lights, the following four questions should be asked:

1. Do I need them?
2. How much light do I need?
3. When do I need it?
4. What color can it be?

Here are some ways to reduce light pollution and save wildlife:

- Turn off unnecessary lights outside your house at night. Consider using motion-sensor lights that only turn on when necessary. Choose the minimum intensity of bulb required. If you can use LED lights, choose a warm color (yellow or amber) rather than blue.

- Make sure outside lights are shielded so they direct light downward. If you live in an apartment building, check the outside lighting. If it is not shielded, ask how a change can be made. Move lamps away from windows, and close blinds or curtains to keep the light inside.

- Be kind to fireflies. If you have a backyard or a cottage, park or empty lot that you visit, you may be able to create a safe haven for fireflies. Hint: Fireflies like litter around trees and an occasional rotten log for their larvae.

- Shiny polished surfaces like tin-roofed sheds, cars and asphalt reflect light, contribute to skyglow and create light spillage into unwanted areas. Dark surfaces are better than white. Check the outdoor features around your home or apartment to reduce your personal light-pollution footprint.

- Make your area more ecologically friendly for migratory birds and diurnal animals. Talk to your neighbors about reviving the natural night in the surrounding ecosystem. Even shielded lights have ecological consequences. Shutting them off is a better way to restore the natural environment.

Several species of Wisconsin birds share the bird bath in this garden and pollinate the wildflowers. The world population is approaching eight billion people—we must learn to live in harmony with nature. CHRISTINLOLA/DREAMSTIME.COM

You can come to love the night as I have. Listen to the sounds of the night with an adult family member who shares your love of the night. Establish a sit spot and listen to the sounds that surround you. Soon you will be hearing night crickets, frogs, birds and many other dark-loving animals singing deep into the night. Scents stay closer to the ground in the cool night air, so you can smell the richness of the night too. The light-dark cycle is natural on our planet, and saving it is only a light switch away. Take a walk on the dark side. Be a part of the effort to bring back the night and help conserve the earth's living species and ecosystems.

Many states are passing bills to protect "dark-sky places" as they become rarer and ever more remote. Thousands of visitors go to these locations every year to enjoy a glimpse into the marvels of our universe. CONSTANTIN OPRIS/DREAMSTIME.COM

Resources

Print

Bogard, Paul. *The End of Night: Searching for Natural Darkness in an Age of Artificial Light.* Back Bay Books, 2014.

Galat, Joan Marie. *Dark Matters: Nature's Reaction to Light Pollution.* Red Deer Press, 2017.

Harrison, David L. *After Dark: Poems about Nocturnal Animals.* Wordsong, 2020.

Wolfson, Elissa, and Margaret A. Barker. *Audubon Birding Adventures for Kids: Activities and Ideas for Watching, Feeding, and Housing Our Feathered Friends.* Cool Springs Press, 2020.

Online

Bat Conservation International: batcon.org
*Dedicated to conserving the world's bats and their ecosystems

Dark Sky Meter: darkskymeter.com
*I have a Dark Sky Meter app on my phone. It uses the camera to measure the darkness of the sky wherever I am in the world. The data is then uploaded to a server that generates a global light-pollution map online that is used for scientific research.

Dark Sky Preserves: space.com/international-dark-sky-preserves-night-sky-sites-tour.html
*Dark-sky preserves around the world that protect the night sky

Fatal Light Awareness Program: flap.org
*A Canadian charity protecting birds from building collisions

International Dark-Sky Association: darksky.org

*The IDA is one of the largest and most active groups protecting night skies in the world.

IDA and the **National Audubon Society:** darksky.org/what-you-should-know-about-bird-migration-and-light-pollution

*A collaboration between Audubon's mission to protect birds and the IDA's mandate to protect the night

Loss of the Night: myskyatnight.com

*A web application to share and visualize skyglow data from citizen scientists

Mont-Mégantic International Dark Sky Reserve: darksky.org/our-work/conservation/idsp/reserves/montmegantic

*Dark Sky Place of the Year 2021. Through collaboration, an entire region is an island of darkness with better access to the stars above.

Glossary

airglow—the natural glow of the earth's atmosphere

aurora australis—the southern lights, a natural, multicolored light display visible in the sky of the southern hemisphere

aurora borealis—the northern lights, a natural, multicolored light display visible in the sky of the northern hemisphere

biofluorescence—light absorbed by living organisms at one wavelength and emitted at a different wavelength, causing them to glow

bioluminescent—a description of organisms that emit light due to biochemical reactions; seen in fireflies, glow worms and deep-sea fish

carcinogenic—a substance or activity having the potential to cause cancer

circadian clock—the 24-hour cycle of biological processes, reset on a daily basis

citizen science—the gathering and studying of data by the collective power of people

constellations—collections of stars seen by people on Earth as figures or patterns

dinoflagellates—single-celled aquatic organisms with two tail-like flagella

dormant state—a multiday sleeplike state that hibernating animals go into to survive cold winters

echolocation—a technique for locating objects using high-frequency sound waves

ecosystems—communities of living organisms interacting with each other and their nonliving environment

fledglings—young birds that have just developed their flight feathers

herbivore—an organism, big or small, that feeds mostly on plants

insectivorous—feeding on insects, worms and other invertebrates

invertebrates—animals that do not have a vertebral column or backbone, comprising 90 percent of all living animal species

light-year—the distance traveled by light in one year, which at 186,000 miles per second is about 6 trillion miles (9.5 trillion kilometers)

molting—the shedding of an outer layer of horns, skin, feathers or hair to make way for new growth

nocturnal—most active at night

photic zone—the surface layer of a body of water in which photosynthesis is possible

photoperiod—the duration of daily natural light an organism receives

photophore—a tiny light-producing organ found in some fish and other animals

photosynthesis—the process green plants use to convert sunlight into their own food

phototaxis—the movement of an organism toward or away from a light source

physiological—relating to the way that living organisms and their systems work

planetarium—a "sky theater" in which a device projects a simulation of the night sky onto a domed ceiling

polarized light—light waves vibrating in a single direction; occurs when light bounces off reflective surfaces

raptor—a meat-eating bird of prey like a hawk, eagle or vulture, with a hooked beak and large, strong talons on its feet

symbiotic—characterized by a cooperative relationship, such as two or more organisms living and working together to help each other

thermal-imaging cameras—devices that translate heat energy into visible light so that images of objects can be seen and captured in low light

ungulates—hoofed mammals such as deer, moose, horses and elephants

vertebrates—animals with a spinal column and a skeleton made of cartilage and bone; examples are humans, birds and snakes

wildlife corridor—an area or passageway that connects wildlife habitats and populations that have been separated by roadways or developments

zodiacal light—sunlight reflecting off interplanetary dust

Index

*Page numbers in **bold** indicate an image caption.*

Index (continued)

Acknowledgments

Thank you, Kirstie Hudson and the Orca team, for holding me steady and true as this journey moved from page to page through the night. Special thanks to the design team for their stellar job designing a book on this difficult subject. To my agent, Stacey Kondla, you are the compass in my literary pilgrimage.

It has been an eye-opener meeting and working with talented photographers who tackle the difficulties of capturing images at night. Thank you, Travis Longcore and Catherine Rich, for reviewing the manuscript, cross-checking the science and providing your suggestions. Thanks to sweet Reta for her natural luminance.

Finally, a bow of respect to all the night-loving creatures in the natural world who make our spinning planet so delightfully habitable.

ELLEN REITMAN

STEPHEN AITKEN

is a biologist, artist and science writer who has been creating children's books for the past 15 years. Stephen's books and articles are inspired by the wonders of the natural world. He has explored the forests, oceans and mountaintops of the world at all times of the day and night. Stephen is the co-founder and executive secretary of the charity Biodiversity Conservancy International and senior editor of the journal *Biodiversity*. He lives in Ottawa.